LIFE IN COLONIAL AMERICA

THE COUNTRYSIDE IN COLONIAL AMERICA

GEORGE CAPACCIO

Cavendish
Square

New York

Published in 2015 by Cavendish Square Publishing, LLC
243 5th Avenue, Suite 136, New York, NY 10016

Copyright © 2015 by Cavendish Square Publishing, LLC

First Edition

Website: cavendishsq.com

This publication represents the opinions and views of the author based on his or her personal experience, knowledge, and research. The information in this book serves as a general guide only. The author and publisher have used their best efforts in preparing this book and disclaim liability rising directly or indirectly from the use and application of this book.

CPSIA Compliance Information: Batch # WS14CSQ

All websites were available and accurate when this book was sent to press.

Library of Congress Cataloging-in-Publication Data
Capaccio, George.
The countryside in colonial america / George Capaccio.
pages cm. — (Life in colonial America)
Includes index.
ISBN 978-1-62712-885-8 (hardcover) ISBN 978-1-62712-887-2 (ebook)
1. United States—History—Colonial period, ca. 1600-1775—Juvenile literature. 2. Indians of North America—History—Colonial period, ca. 1600-1775—Juvenile literature. I. Title.
E188.C26 2014
973.2—dc23
2014006063

Editorial Director: Dean Miller
Editor: Fletcher Doyle
Senior Copy Editor: Wendy A. Reynolds
Art Director: Jeffrey Talbot
Designer: Joseph Macri
Production Editor: David McNamara
Production Manager: Jennifer Ryder-Talbot

The photographs in this book are used by permission through the courtesy of: Cover photo by David Sucsy/E+/Getty Images; © North Wind/North Wind Picture Archives, 4; © North Wind/North Wind Picture Archives, 5; Bridgeman Art Library/Getty Images, 6; Picture History/Newscom, 8; Universal History Archive/Universal Images Group/Getty Images, 9; © North Wind/North Wind Picture Archives, 13; Walden69/File:Early_indian_east.jpg/Wikimedia Commons, 14; © North Wind/North Wind Picture Archives, 16; © North Wind/North Wind Picture Archives, 18–19; Print Collector/Hulton Archive/Getty Images, 20; Marilyn Angel Wynn/Nativestock/Getty Images, 21; Marilyn Angel Wynn/Nativestock/Getty Images, 21; Angel Wynn/DanitaDelimont.com "Danita Delimont Photography"/Newscom, 23; © North Wind/North Wind Picture Archives, 24; DEA PICTURE LIBRARY/De Agostini Picture Library/Getty Images, 26; © North Wind/North Wind Picture Archives, 27; Bridgeman Art Library/Getty Images, 29; © North Wind/North Wind Picture Archives, 30; Time Life Pictures/The LIFE Picture Collection/Getty Images, 33; SuperStock/Getty Images, 34; Antonio Gisbert/The Bridgeman Art Library/Getty Images, 36; Nikater/File:Wampanoag2.jpg/Wikimedia Commons, 39; © North Wind Picture Archives/The Image Works, 40; © North Wind/North Wind Picture Archives, 42; © North Wind/North Wind Picture Archives, 44; © North Wind/North Wind Picture Archives, 45; © North Wind/North Wind Picture Archives, 45; Marcela/File:Turnspit Dog Working.jpg/Wikimedia Commons, 47; © North Wind/North Wind Picture Archives, 48; © North Wind/North Wind Picture Archives, 48; © Bruno Monico/Shutterstock.com, 49; © Zhukov Oleg/Shutterstock.com, 50; Weson/File:Triangular trade.jpg/Wikimedia Commons, 51; © North Wind/North Wind Picture Archives, 52; © North Wind/North Wind Picture Archives, 54; © North Wind/North Wind Picture Archives, 55; © North Wind/North Wind Picture Archives, 56; © North Wind/North Wind Picture Archives, 58; The Bridgeman Art Library/Getty Images, 60; Ekely/E+/Getty Images, 61; © Madlen/Shutterstock.com, 63; © North Wind/North Wind Picture Archives, 64; © North Wind/North Wind Picture Archives, 65; © Heritage Image Partnership Ltd/Alamy, 66.

Printed in the United States of America

Contents

INTRODUCTION

In Search of a Better Life

In the opening decades of the seventeenth century, shiploads of **immigrants** crossed the Atlantic to reach their destination in North America. Some came to escape religious persecution, some in search of riches, and some for economic opportunity that was not available in their home countries. These are among the things that led them to take a voyage that was long and dangerous, with few comforts. Many died during the voyage from disease. Many ships went down in Atlantic storms.

The earliest voyages were planned and financed by private British businesses like the Virginia Company and the Massachusetts Bay Company. Based in London, these companies wanted to profit from colonial settlements. They negotiated contracts with prospective settlers in the British colonies, most of whom couldn't afford the move. In exchange for the cost of transportation and start-up expenses in the colony, settlers agreed to work for the company without pay, usually for a period of four to seven years. On paper, this sounded like a good deal. In practice, colonial governors sometimes violated the terms of the contract and forced settlers to continue working as servants of the company.

Severe forms of punishment were used to enforce obedience. A settler convicted of even a minor offense might be whipped, shot, hung, or even burned alive.

For most of the seventeenth century, immigrants settled along the coastal region between Maine and South Carolina (Georgia wasn't founded until 1733). Daunting obstacles discouraged people from moving deeper into the interior of the continent. One such obstacle was the Appalachian Mountains, which extend for almost 2,000 miles (3,200 kilometers) and separate the eastern coastal plains from the interior lowlands. Another obstacle was the lack of an easily navigable river into the interior. The St. Lawrence River in Canada could have carried settlers westward, but the French controlled the river, and France was one of England's longstanding enemies.

The communities that developed in British North America were relatively isolated. Each was dependent on trade with Europe for essential items and as markets for their products. In addition, each colony had its own port, which made cross-Atlantic trade feasible. Life in colonial America was mainly rural. Most people lived as farmers.

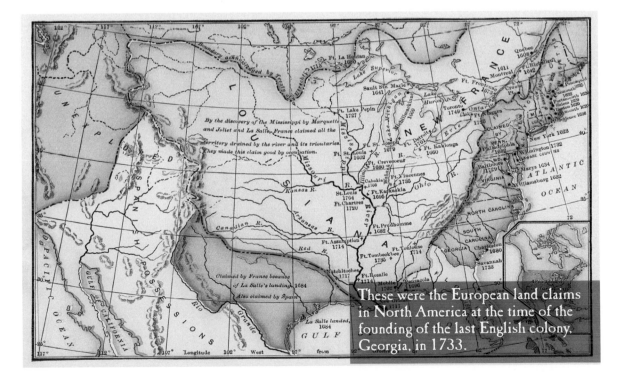

These were the European land claims in North America at the time of the founding of the last English colony, Georgia, in 1733.

CHAPTER ONE

Struggle for Survival

The departure of the *Mayflower* from England was delayed until September, pushing its arrival in North America back to November.

"Wednesday, the sixth of September, the winds coming east north east, a fine small gale, we loosed from Plymouth, having been kindly entertained and courteously used by divers friends there dwelling, and after many difficulties in boisterous storms, at length, by God's providence, upon the ninth of November following, by break of the day we espied land which was deemed to be Cape Cod, and so afterward it proved."

— Mourt's Relation: A Journal of the Pilgrims at Plymouth, 1620

The Pilgrims who settled what is now Massachusetts were beset by problems from the start. They twice had their departure from England delayed by leaks in the *Speedwell*, which was to join the *Mayflower* for the trip to the Virginia colony. The *Speedwell* was repaired once in July and once in August before the decision was made to leave it behind and place all people and supplies aboard the *Mayflower*. This delayed their departure until September.

The nine-and-a-half week voyage was then plagued by storms for more than half of its duration. When they did reach North America, they missed their mark, arriving at Cape Cod instead of the mouth of the Hudson River, which at that time was part of the Virginia colony. They tried to sail south, but storms pushed them back toward Cape Cod and the Pilgrims decided to go no farther.

The length of the voyage pushed their arrival into November, exposing the homeless travelers to the cold and preventing them from gathering any food that might help them get through the winter.

MARY CHILTON

Legend has it that Mary Chilton was the first female to step ashore on Plymouth Rock. While there is no evidence to validate this story, it has been a treasured part of the Chilton family history. Mary was twelve or thirteen when she is supposed to have touched her foot down on the famous rock. "The Landing of the Pilgrims," painted in 1877 by Henry Bacon, celebrates Mary's legendary arrival. She came aboard the *Mayflower* with her parents, both of whom died within a short time of each other that first winter. Historians have yet to discover which Pilgrim family raised Mary after her parents passed away.

Mary Chilton is reputed to be the first woman to step foot ashore at Plymouth.

On the *Mayflower*, only twenty-eight of the 102 passengers were women, and three of them were pregnant.

While at sea, Elizabeth Hopkins gave birth to a son, Oceanus, who was named after his birthplace. With the *Mayflower* anchored off Cape Cod, Susanna White also gave birth to a boy, who was named Peregrine.

Peregrine White lived to be eighty, but Oceanus died during the first winter spent by the Pilgrims in the New World. The third pregnant woman, Mary Norris Allerton, didn't survive childbirth. Her baby was stillborn.

BASKETS OF INDIAN CORN BUT NO SIGNS OF LIFE

The Pilgrims reached Cape Cod harbor needing food and shelter. In his journal, the future governor of Plymouth Colony, William Bradford, describes what it was like for the passengers to arrive at their destination:

> "... they had now no friends to welcome them, nor inns to entertain or refresh their weather-beaten bodies, no houses or much less towns to repair to ... And for the season it was winter, and they that know the winters of that country know them to be sharp and violent and subject to cruel and fierce storms, dangerous to travel to known places, much more to search an unknown coast. Besides, what could they see but a hideous and desolate wilderness, full of wild beasts and wild men? and what multitudes there might be of them they knew not ... For summer being done, all things stand upon them with a weather-beaten face; and the whole country, full of woods and thickets, represented a wild and savage hew ..."

After their long voyage, the Pilgrims were desperate to find food. A group of well-armed men, while searching the coast, came upon a deserted Native American village. Edward Winslow, one of the Pilgrim leaders, gives this eyewitness account of what the search party discovered:

Edward Winslow kept a journal of the early days of the Plymouth colony.

"Passing thus a field or two, which were not great, we came to another which had also been new gotten, and there we found where a house had been, and four or five old planks laid together; also we found a great kettle which had been some ship's kettle and brought out of Europe. There was also a heap of sand ... which we [dug] up, and in it we found a little old basket full of fair Indian corn, and [dug] further and found a fine great new basket full of very fair corn of this year, with some thirty-six goodly ears of corn, some yellow, some red, and others mixed with blue, which was a very goodly sight ... We were in suspense what to do with it and the kettle, and at length ... we concluded to take the kettle and as much of the corn as we could carry away with us; and when our shallop came, if we could find any of the people, and come to parley with them, we would give them the kettle again, and satisfy them for their corn ..."

In December, the Pilgrims settled on a location for the community they planned to build. They called their new British colony Plymouth; the site was a deserted village that had belonged to the Patuxet people. Without enough food and adequate shelter, the colonists struggled to survive their first New England winter—while members of another tribe, the Wampanoag, kept their distance, watching how the newcomers were coping. By spring, only half of the original 102 *Mayflower* passengers were still alive. The rest had died from hunger, disease, and exposure to the cold.

The early settlers also had to survive war with the Native Americans, but those who came within sight of America's east coast must have been filled with a deep sense of relief and awe. One colonist who recorded his earliest impressions of this new land wrote, "The air at twelve leagues' distance smelt as sweet as a new-blown garden."

Along the eastern coast, thick forests teemed with wildlife. Streams and rivers were home to innumerable species of fish and waterfowl. Captain John Smith, who helped establish the British colony of Virginia, wrote, "Heaven and earth never agreed better to frame a place for man's habitation."

REGIONAL DIFFERENCES

A variety of motivations and geographical features affected the differences among the colonies in terms of their character and customs. For instance, English **Puritans** migrated to New England for the freedom to practice their interpretation of Christianity.

Because of that region's rocky soil and colder climate, many colonists turned to the sea for their livelihood. The Puritans tended to live close together in towns and to operate small farms. These tightly knit communities provided them with protection from hostile tribes and allowed them to construct three essential buildings in close proximity: the church, the inn or tavern, and the fort, otherwise known as a **blockhouse**.

ATTACK ON DEERFIELD

At different periods during the 1700s, British and French armies, along with their Native American allies, fought for control of North America. The town of Deerfield in Massachusetts was a British settlement. Fearing an attack by the French, Deerfield colonists stayed within the town's protective fence. However, on February 29, 1704, several hundred French and Native American fighters staged a raid. They killed some fifty civilians and took more than 100 captives, leading them on a forced march to Canada. About one year later, most of the captives returned home safely. Some stayed behind, choosing to become part of either French or Native American society.

THE MIDDLE COLONIES

Before the English became the dominant presence in New York, the area was settled by the Dutch, who brought their customs with them, including their enjoyment of competitive games such as bowling. Most of the settlers in New York were farmers, owing to the rich, fertile soil in this region.

Quakers predominated in Pennsylvania and western New Jersey. Pennsylvania's tolerant government drew a great variety of religious groups or denominations. Besides Quakers, these included Lutherans, Presbyterians, Moravians, Baptists, Methodists, Roman Catholics, and Episcopalians. Settlers tended to form their own communities based on their particular religion or ethnic identity.

Southern Colonies

In the South, with its longer growing seasons, the emphasis was on cash crops. Wealthy planters established large **plantations** close to rivers in order to more conveniently transport their crops to seaside ports for shipment overseas. The major export crop was tobacco.

Maryland and Virginia operated under a system by which a plantation owner was given fifty acres for every worker they could import. These workers were called **indentured servants**, and they worked for a period of usually five years, receiving only room and board. After they finished their time of servitude, they were to be paid a prearranged bonus of money or land, called "freedom dues."

This practice created many large plantations, which kept much of the region rural and discouraged the development of cities. Without population centers, there was no need to build schools. The lack of cities also meant there was no place to develop a professional class of lawyers and doctors, or a middle class of businessmen. As a result, the gap in wealth between the large landowners and the workers was much higher than in the North.

Plantations were similar in some respects to villages, as they had barns, stables, shacks for servants or African American slaves, and large sheds where the cut tobacco was cured. The children of the wealthy were educated on the plantation by tutors.

There were two problems faced by the indentured servants. Only about 40 percent of them survived their time of servitude. If they did survive, they discovered that so much land had been given away to the plantation owners that, once they gained their freedom, they were forced to farm in the less fertile western regions at the foot of the mountains. They were less protected from Native American attacks in the western areas. They could not afford to own slaves or indentured servants, and struggled to raise enough to feed their families.

Many poor whites and African Americans, some of whom had been indentured servants, joined in what is called Bacon's Rebellion in 1676. Organized by Nathaniel Bacon, the fight evolved into a battle over control of the government of Virginia. Bacon burned Jamestown to the ground, but was eventually defeated.

This rebellion helped convince the planters to abandon the practice of importing indentured servants, which had made them wealthy, and they turned instead, by 1680, to importing slaves.

Survival rates were poor for the indentured servants who cultivated tobacco in colonial Virginia.

By the time of the American Revolution in 1775, two centuries of colonization resulted in a population of roughly 2.5 million people in the British colonies. Most of them, about 58 percent, were of European descent. About half a million African Americans lived throughout the colonies, mostly as slaves, though some had secured their freedom or worked as indentured servants.

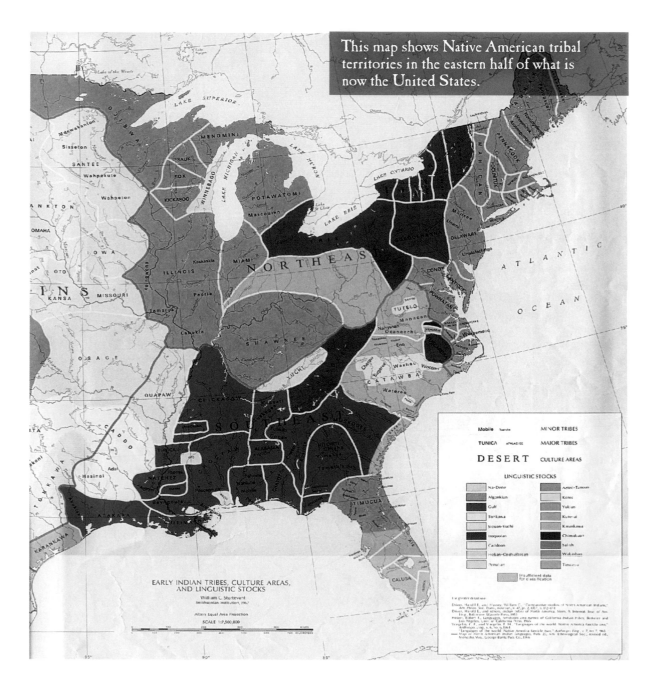

This map shows Native American tribal territories in the eastern half of what is now the United States.

EARLY INDIAN TRIBES, CULTURE AREAS, AND LINGUISTIC STOCKS

William C. Sturtevant
Smithsonian Institution, 1967

Albers Equal Area Projection
SCALE 1:7,500,000

Most of the colonists were farmers and planters living in small, rural settlements or communities. Cities were small—in fact, none had more than 40,000 residents. They were also few and far between; only five percent of the population in the 1700s lived in cities. The four largest cities at the time of the American Revolution were Philadelphia, New York, Boston, and Charleston, South Carolina.

People typically didn't travel too far from their homes. Much of the land was forested, the weather could turn hazardous, and there was the constant threat of attack by the indigenous people. Isolation forced these communities to become self-sufficient. It also encouraged them to fear outsiders, whether Native Americans, French and Spanish intruders, or neighboring colonists.

During the first three quarters of the seventeenth century, most of the settlers came from England. Therefore British culture shaped the overall character of the colonies, class structure, customs, and language. After 1680, however, more people from continental Europe began migrating to North America, including people from Germany, Switzerland, France, Scotland, and Ireland. As the diversity of this immigrant wave increased, something uniquely American slowly began to emerge—a new kind of society composed of people from different cultural backgrounds finding ways to live together in a new land.

Immigrants to the colonies also encountered the original inhabitants of the entire coastal region. At the beginning of the seventeenth century, tens of thousands of Native Americans made their homes in the eastern part of what would one day become the United States. Their territory reached eastward from the Mississippi River to the Atlantic Ocean, and included the area around the Great Lakes. The many tribes that lived in this vast region included the Huron, Shawnee, Ojibwa, Mohawk, Powhatan, Abenaki, and Wampanoag. Since their land was mostly covered with dense forests, they are collectively known as the Eastern Woodland Native Americans.

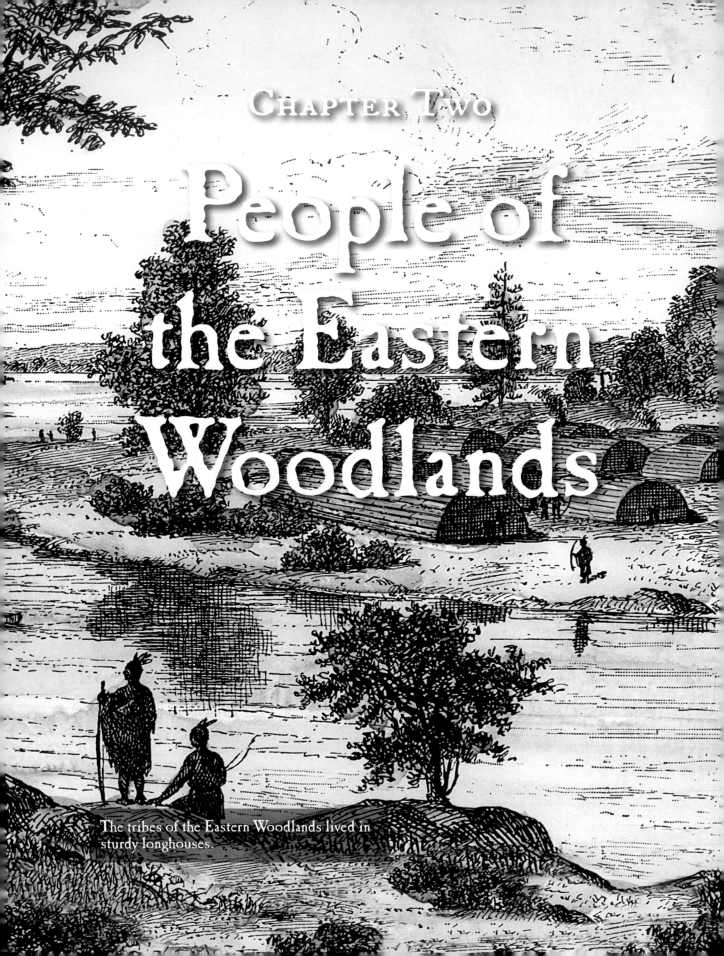

CHAPTER TWO

People of the Eastern Woodlands

The tribes of the Eastern Woodlands lived in sturdy longhouses.

"I took aim with my arquebus and shot straight at one of the three chiefs, and with this shot two fell to the ground and one of their companions was wounded who died thereof a little later. I had put four bullets into my arquebus... The Iroquois were much astonished that two men should have been killed so quickly, although they were provided with shields made of cotton thread woven together and wood, which were proof against their arrows."
—From *The Works of Samuel de Champlain*, describing a June 1609 battle in which some Native Americans were introduced to European weapons.

The Eastern Woodland Native Americans, though organized into distinct tribes and tribal groups, shared a common culture. Most of the tribes, for instance, depended on the forest for much of their food. Women gathered berries, wild fruit, and edible nuts. The men hunted game and fished in the rivers and streams. Woodland Native Americans ate venison and used deer hides to make clothing and footwear, antlers to make arrowheads, and hooves to make glue.

Unlike the Cheyenne, the Sioux, and other migratory tribes of the Great Plains, Eastern Woodland tribes were settled people. Rather than uprooting themselves and traveling to different hunting grounds, they lived in stable villages and devoted much of their time to farming. With their knowledge of agriculture, the Woodland Native Americans were able to grow life-sustaining crops of corn, beans, squash, and other hearty vegetables.

The Longhouse

Eastern Woodland Native Americans built sturdy homes known as **longhouses**. These structures were long, narrow, and rectangular. Their size varied, depending on the number of families who would live in them.

The northeastern region of the United States is the ancestral home of the Iroquois, and their longhouses reveal much not only about the Iroquois but also about Eastern Woodland culture. The word "Iroquois" is a French term referring to a group of six related Native American tribes or nations: the Senecas, Mohawks, Oneidas, Onondagas, Cayugas, and Tuscaroras. (Originally, there were five nations. But in the early eighteenth century the Tuscaroras joined the confederacy.) The people of the Six Nations know themselves not as the Iroquois, but as *Hau de no sau nee* (ho dee noe sho nee), which translates to "People Building a Longhouse."

The structures built by the Iroquois could be longer than a football field.

To the Iroquois, the longhouse was a dwelling and a symbol of their culture. They envisioned the land in which they lived as one enormous longhouse in which each of the Six Nations served a purpose. Many historians regard the original Iroquois Confederacy as one of the world's oldest participatory democracies. The principles and ideals upon which this union was founded inspired the leaders of the American Revolution—men like Benjamin Franklin and Thomas Jefferson—who struggled to create a United States in which the government reflected the will of the people, as it did in the Iroquois Confederacy.

The average Iroquois longhouse was 180 to 220 feet (55 to 67 meters) long, though some were longer than a football field. Regardless of length, most were about 20 feet (6 m) wide and 20 feet (6 m) high. They were made of poles and branches and covered with sheets of bark. The size of a longhouse depended

An Algonquin village, as observed by the English expedition under John White in 1585, was built inside a protective palisade.

ANOTHER LOOK AT EASTERN WOODLAND DWELLINGS

Samuel de Champlain (1567–1635) was a French explorer. Among his many notable achievements, he founded the Canadian city of Quebec and explored the eastern Great Lakes in the early 1600s. An excerpt from his journal, originally written in French, describes the Iroquois longhouses he came upon:

"Their lodges ... are fashioned like ... arbors, covered with tree-bark, twenty-five to thirty fathoms long more or less, and six wide, leaving in the middle a passage from ten to twelve feet wide which runs from one end to the other. On both sides is a sort of platform, four feet in height, on which they sleep in summer to escape the annoyance of fleas of which they have many, and in winter they lie beneath on mats near the fire in order to be warmer than on top of the platform. They gather a supply of dry wood and fill their cabins with it, to burn in winter, and at the end of these cabins is a space where they keep their Indian corn, which they put in great casks, made of tree-bark, in the middle of their lodge ...

Pieces of wood are suspended on which they put their clothes, provisions and other things for fear of mice which are in great numbers. In one such cabin there will be twelve fires, which make twenty-four households, and there is smoke in good earnest, causing many to have great eye troubles, to which they are subject, even towards the end of their lives losing their sight; for there is no window nor opening except in the roof of their cabins by which, the smoke can escape ...

They sometimes change their village site after ten, twenty, or thirty years, and move it one, two or three leagues from the former spot, if they are not forced by their enemies to decamp and move to a greater distance ..."

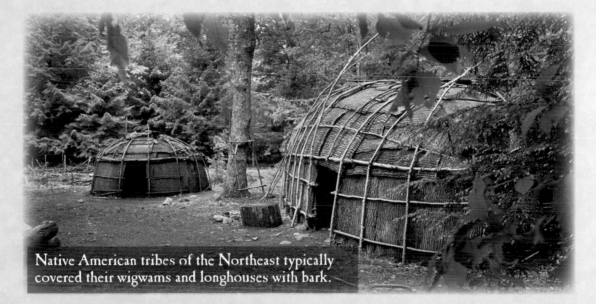

Native American tribes of the Northeast typically covered their wigwams and longhouses with bark.

Sleeping platforms lined the interior of traditional Iroquois longhouses, such as this one in the village of Kanata on the Six Nations of the Grand River Reserve, Ohsweken, Ontario, Canada.

on the size of the extended family for which it was built. An extended family included parents, grandparents, children, aunts and uncles, and cousins. One longhouse might be home for as many as twenty families related through the mother's side.

The families living in a longhouse belonged to the same **clan**, which used an animal or bird as its symbol. Members of a clan were considered relatives, and therefore were not allowed to marry. Young people could only marry someone from a different clan. The Iroquois society was **matriarchal**, and the leaders of each clan were women. They determined which men would represent their clan at the tribal council. Women also were in charge of farming and making sure each family had its fair share of food.

The Wampanoag Wetuash

Of the 102 passengers aboard the *Mayflower* in 1620, about forty were Protestant Separatists. All identified themselves as "**Saints,**" but today we refer to them as "Pilgrims." In their native England, they had suffered religious persecution. They came to North America in order to establish a colony where they could practice their religion without fear of repression.

For more than a month, small bands of Pilgrims explored Cape Cod in search of a suitable place to build their colony. During one such exploration, the men discovered some Native American dwellings.

The houses belonged to Wampanoag families. The Wampanoag had been living in this region for more than 10,000 years at the time of the Pilgrims' arrival. Their tribal name means "People of the Dawn," or "People of the First Light." In the Wampanoag language, the word for house or dwelling is **wetu**. (The plural is **wetuash**.) A small, single-family wetu was dome-shaped, about 15 feet (4.5 m) across, and 8 to 10 feet (2 m to 3 m) high. Husbands and wives, working together, built these dwellings out of bent saplings covered with sheets of birch bark or mats made of reeds.

The Wampanoag called their dome-shaped shelter a wetu.

During the spring and summer, the Wampanoag lived along the coast where they fished and farmed. After the autumn harvest, they moved inland to hunting camps far from blustery Atlantic storms. Protected by the surrounding forest, the men hunted deer, moose, bear, and game birds such as wild turkey, and fished in frozen lakes and streams by cutting holes in the ice.

During the colder months, extended Wampanoag families lived in long-houses, or *nush weetu*, which were similar to those of the Iroquois people. Longhouses could be 50 to 60 feet (15 m to 18 m) in length and accommodate as many fifty family members.

CHAPTER THREE

Jamestown and the Powhatan People

The tribes ruled by Powhatan lived in villages and farmed, sending small groups to the sea in the summer to fish.

"This was that time, which still to this day we called the
starving time; it were too vile to say, and scarce to be beleeved,
what we endured: but the occasion was our owne, for want of
providence, industrie and government, and not the barrennesse
and defect of the Countrie..."
—From John Smith, *The Generall Historie of Virginia,*
New England & The Summer Isles

In 1492, the Italian explorer Christopher Columbus mistook the islands of
the Caribbean for India, and called the inhabitants "Indians." Five years
later, the Italian-born John Cabot (whose original name was Giovanni
Caboto) led the first group of English explorers to North America.
However, it wasn't until 1607 that the English attempted to plant a permanent
colony in what Europeans called the "New World." They named this settlement
Jamestown in honor of James I, the new King of England.

"... some of his people led us to their houses, showed us the growing of their
Corne & the maner of setting it, gave us Tobacco, Wallnutes, mullberyes,
strawberryes, and Respises. One shewed us the herbe called in their tongue
wisacan, which they say heales poysoned woundes, it is like lyverwort of
bloudwort. One gaue me a Roote wherewith they poison their Arrowes. they
would shew us any thing we Demaunded, and laboured very much by signes
to make us understand their Languadg."
— excerpt from the journal of one of the original Jamestown colonists

In December 1606, 105 colonists—all men— departed from England aboard three ships: the *Susan Constant*, *Godspeed*, and *Discovery*. The leader of this expedition was Captain Christopher Newport. Also on board was Captain John Smith, an accomplished explorer, soldier, mapmaker, and author who would eventually govern Jamestown. After several grueling months at sea, the ships arrived at Chesapeake Bay in April 1607. From there, they sailed about 60 miles (96 km) up the James River, which, like the colony, they named after the English king. The settlers chose a site that would conceal their whereabouts from hostile Spanish explorers. The site also provided deep water in which to anchor their ships. The following day, the passengers went ashore and began the task of building a colony.

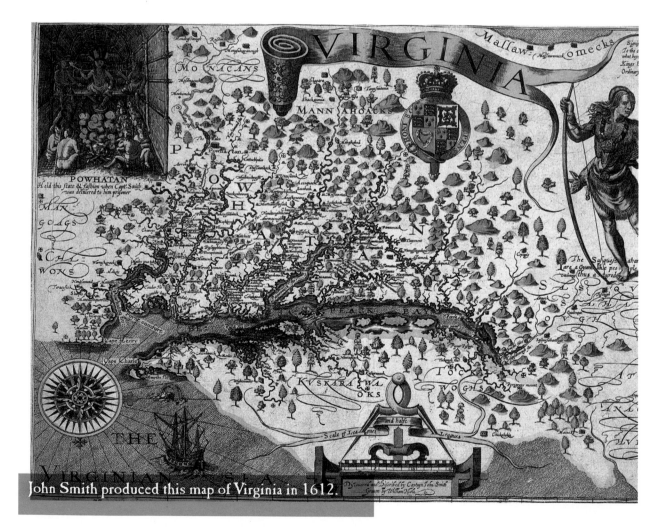

John Smith produced this map of Virginia in 1612.

THE COUNTRYSIDE IN COLONIAL AMERICA

Captain John Smith and the tribes of the Chesapeake clashed because of misunderstandings.

POWHATAN, A POWERFUL LEADER

What they did not know was that their isolated outpost was located in the midst of a Native American chiefdom consisting of some thirty Eastern Woodland tribes. The members of these tribes all spoke a dialect of the Algonquian language and were ruled by one very powerful man—Powhatan, whose favorite daughter was Pocahontas.

Collectively, the tribes under his leadership were known as the Powhatan people. Like other Eastern Woodland Native Americans, they lived in villages of twenty to thirty longhouses suitable for one hundred or more people. During the spring and summer, they moved in small groups to the seashore to fish. In late summer, they returned to their villages to prepare for the coming winter by harvesting beans, squash, and corn.

When the English colony of Jamestown was founded in 1607, Powhatan was already in his sixties. A shrewd leader and a man of great authority, he worked hard to keep the tribes from warring against each other and thus destroying the chiefdom.

Powhatan lived in the village of Werowocomoco on the York River in eastern Virginia. Because of his status, he had many servants, forty bodyguards, and one hundred wives whose personal needs were provided for by villages under his rule. Powhatan was well aware of the English colonists settling on the James River. But instead of declaring war on them, he hoped to enlist them in his fight against rival inland tribes. Powhatan admired the superior technology of the English, especially their weapons and tools. He knew how dangerous these weapons were and had no intention of provoking the English. It would be much easier for him to subdue his enemies if he made these newcomers his allies and trading partners.

Mutual Misunderstanding Leads to Conflict

Powhatan conspired to contain the English by drawing them into the intertribal coalition he had created. It seems that both sides seriously misjudged the other. While the Native Americans thought they could control and **subjugate** the settlers, the settlers in turn thought their neighbors were nothing more than brute savages. Furthermore, the early colonists in Jamestown wrongly believed they could turn the Powhatan people into obedient laborers and servants.

Converting the Native people of Virginia to Anglican Christianity was one of the stated goals of the Virginia Company of London, the organization that sponsored the Jamestown colony and its initial settlers. The men who started the colony were more interested in becoming rich, however. They hoped to unearth gold and other precious metals in Virginia's wilderness.

One thing that they weren't prepared to do was get their hands dirty producing the crops they would need to survive. Many of the colonists belonged to England's **aristocracy**. Working with their hands had never been part of their lives. A second group of colonists consisted of out-of-work men from the streets of London who knew how to beg and steal, but next to nothing about farming.

The promoters who were eager to recruit settlers for the colony had assured the British public that the locals were generous and docile. According to these promoters, the indigenous people would recognize the superiority of the colonists and easily submit to them. If they refused to submit, then they would be violating God's will since God had meant for the English to transform the Virginia wilderness into productive farmland. Having been told this, the Jamestown colonists expected the Native Americans to supply them with food whenever necessary.

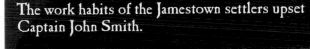
The work habits of the Jamestown settlers upset Captain John Smith.

Whatever their intended goals, the settlers spent most of their time searching for gold instead of building a self-sustaining colony. Captain John Smith, who had accompanied the settlers from England, frowned upon their constant search for riches. He wrote: "There was no talke, no hope, no worke, but dig gold, wash gold, [and] refine gold."

Nine months after this first wave of 104 colonists set foot on Virginia soil, only thirty-eight were still alive, killed in battle or by disease and hunger. In the summer, swarms of mosquitoes infected the

Chief Powhatan ruled on the fate of John Smith from his seat of honor inside his longhouse.

POWHATAN

Held this state & fashion when Capt. Smith was deliuered to him prisoner 1607

colonists with malaria. Without adequate sanitation facilities, the men drank untreated water from rivers, which spread dysentery and typhoid fever. One of the colonists had this to say about their water supply: "Our drinke [was] cold water taken out of the River, which was at floud [tide] verie salt[y], at a low tide full of slime and filth, which was the destruction of many of our men."

The mortality rate in this region was high; malaria cut ten years off of life expectancy. Most of the immigrants were single men in their late teens or their early twenties. The first women to arrive came in the winter of 1608; there were two among the 100 new settlers who came from England to reinforce the colony. The lack of women meant that the colony was not growing due to low rates of childbirth. This changed in 1619 when the Virginia Company changed its rules to allow single women to immigrate to Jamestown, which had been nearly an all-male settlement.

Between 1620 and 1622, about 150 women arrived in Jamestown and were auctioned off for a payment in tobacco to their future spouses. The region was hard on all new arrivals. Half of the children born in Maryland and Virginia to the newcomers died before the age of twenty.

INCREASED TENSIONS

Life for the Powhatan people had its share of hard times. They kept minimal possessions, and their food supply lasted only through the winter. By then, there was scant left for emergencies like drought or invasions of crop-destroying insects, and certainly not enough to sustain a colony of hungry Englishmen. According to historian Alan Taylor, "What [the English] didn't understand was that the Indians could barely feed themselves and when pressed for more than they had, they became angry."

Taylor recounts an episode in which seventeen Jamestown colonists traveled to a Powhatan village in order to obtain food. Apparently outraged by the colonists' insolent behavior, the men in the village killed all seventeen and stuffed the mouths of the dead colonists with corn. Pressure on Powhatan's food supply from the settlers threatened them with starvation. To make matters worse, settlers sometimes allowed their livestock to wander into Native American cornfields, crushing vital crops. On other occasions, they used their guns to force villagers to give them food.

Despite ongoing conflict between the two groups, Captain John Smith succeeded in trading English goods for food. But that was not enough to keep the settlers' hunger at bay. In September 1608, as the new leader of Jamestown, Smith instituted a policy under which those who refused do their share of work would get nothing to eat. Under his leadership, the men planted corn and dug freshwater wells for drinking.

As a result of these changes, fewer settlers died. But ongoing conflict between settlers and Native Americans showed no sign of decreasing. In December 1607, while Smith and a Native American guide were exploring the Chickahominy River, 200 of Powhatan's men ambushed Smith. For the next two weeks, his captors brought him from one village to another until their journey ended in the village of Powhatan himself.

Captain John Smith—Captive

Accounts of what happened next have left many questions unanswered. According to Smith, who presented different versions of his captivity, the chief had been waiting for him. As Smith entered Powhatan's longhouse, he saw rows of men and women with their heads and shoulders painted red. Tall and commanding, the chief wore a luxurious robe made from raccoon skins. Servants brought food for Captain Smith and while he ate, Powhatan conferred with his advisors, apparently trying to decide what to do with their captive.

Once they made up their minds, two stones were placed at Powhatan's feet. Warriors seized Smith, pushed him to the floor, and forced his head against one of the stones. Smith wrote that the men were: "Being [ready] with their clubs to beat out [my] brains . . ." To prevent this from happening, "Pocahontas the King's dearest daughter" pleaded with her father to spare Smith's life.

In Pursuit of the Real Pocahontas

Much of what we believe about Pocahontas is a myth. Her actual name was Matoaka; "Pocahontas" was a nickname meaning "playful one" or "mischievous one." As a child, she lived with her father and was in her father's household when Smith was brought there as a captive. She probably also accompanied her father's representatives when they visited Jamestown. Historians credit Pocahontas for saving Smith's life in 1609 when he met with Powhatan for the last time. Both leaders were secretly plotting the death of the other even while negotiating the terms of peace between the Native Americans and the colonists. Pocahontas is said to have warned Smith in advance, thus foiling her father's plan.

In 1613, while visiting a friend, Pocahontas was captured and brought to Jamestown as a hostage. It was here that she met colonist John Rolfe. After converting to Christianity, she and Rolfe were married, and Pocahontas became "Rebecca Rolfe." They soon had a son, whom they named Thomas. In 1616 the family went to England where "Rebecca" became something of a celebrity. On the return journey, she passed away from an illness. She was only twenty-one. Her young son stayed in England with her husband's family, while John Rolfe went back to Virginia alone.

Rolfe is credited with introducing tobacco farming to the colony in 1612, thereby guaranteeing its economic survival.

This is the only known portrait of Matoaka, also known as Pocahontas, who was baptized as a Christian and married the Englishman John Rolfe.

The accuracy of the story of Pocahontas saving the life of Captain Smith is in question.

When Powhatan refused, she rushed to his side, "got [my] head in her arms, and laid her own upon [mine] to save [me] from death . . ."

Some scholars argue that Smith may have invented this story since his original account contains no mention of this episode. Scholars also think Smith misinterpreted what was taking place. It's possible the chief had no intention of killing Smith. Rather, he wanted to stage a **mock** execution as a way of demonstrating his power. In any case, Smith was grateful to the chief for sparing his life.

Powhatan apparently misunderstood the meaning of the captain's gratitude. He thought it meant Smith was willing to accept his status as a **subordinate** to Powhatan and his domain. But it meant nothing of the kind. After his release from captivity, Smith returned to Jamestown and continued his efforts to negotiate with the Native Americans for food. Unfortunately, when those efforts failed, he resorted to force, taking food and burning villages.

After Powhatan died in 1618, he was replaced by Opechanganough, who became disenchanted with the expanding colony. In 1622 he launched an attack to try to wipe out the 1,000 settlers now living in Jamestown, killing 347. That set off a war in which the settlers spared only the children so they could convert them to Christianity.

Most of the earliest settlers in Virginia were young white men fleeing poor economic conditions in England; in 1650 they outnumbered women by a ratio of six to one in the Chesapeake region. By 1700, planters in the region had brought about 100,000 of these white men to the area. This represented more than three-quarters of the settlers who came to Maryland and Virginia at the time.

There were only 2,000 people of African descent in Virginia in 1670; this ethnic group made up about seven percent of the 50,000 people who lived in the Southern Colonies. With the increase of the slave trade, by 1750, half of the population of Virginia had come from Africa.

CHAPTER FOUR

Plymouth Plantation and the Wampanoag

The Pilgrims experienced peace with the indigenous people right after their arrival in North America.

"... he tould them also of another Indian whos name was Squanto, a native of this place, who had been in England and could speake better English then him selfe. Being, after some time of entertainmente and gifts, dismist, a while after he came againe, and 5. more with him, and they brought againe all the tooles that were stolen away before, and made way for the coming of their great **Sachem**, called Massasoyt ; who, about 4. or 5. days after, came with the cheefe of his freinds and other attendance, with the aforesaid Squanto. With whom, after frendly entertainment, and some gifts given him, they made a peace with him."
—William Bradford in Of *Plymouth Plantation*

What happened in Jamestown highlights many of the problems in European encounters with Native Americans. In the case of the Pilgrims and the Wampanoag people of Massachusetts, a similar cultural divide was present. Despite several decades of relatively peaceful coexistence, their differences eventually led to King Philip's War (1675–1676). It ended the lives of around one thousand English colonists and about three thousand Native Americans, and destroyed settlements of both.

King Philip was the English name for the leader of the Wamapanoag people. His given name was Metacom, and he was the son of Massasoit. When the Pilgrims disembarked from the *Mayflower* in 1620, Massasoit (like Powhatan in Virginia) ruled over an alliance of Eastern Woodland tribes. The Wampanoag, as part of this alliance, lived in parts of present-day Massachusetts and Rhode Island, including the islands of Martha's Vineyard and Nantucket. (Descendants of the original Wampanoag continue to live in these areas.)

In March 1621, the first formal meeting took place between delegations from the Pilgrims and the Wampanoag. There was no basis for trust, only mutual suspicion. Both sides needed the other, but for somewhat different reasons. The Pilgrims had no natural allies in New England. They needed protection and to learn how to survive in a cold, coastal environment, especially after losing half of their population.

The Wampanoag were vulnerable to attacks from neighboring tribes. Massasoit had once ruled over a confederation of as many as 20,000 people. But by 1620, fewer than 1,000 remained. An alliance with the English, who possessed cannons, muskets, and manpower, would go a long way toward protecting his people. In addition, he hoped to enter into exclusive trading

A Catastrophic Epidemic

The once populous Wampanoag Nation was decimated by the spread of a mysterious disease against which the Native Americans had no immunity. Between 1614 and 1620, a series of **epidemics** wiped out most of the Native American settlements. Estimates put the loss of life at one-third to ninety percent of the local populations. Scientists have speculated about the cause of this epidemic, attributing it to yellow fever, smallpox, plague, and viral hepatitis, among other diseases. A recent study suggests that a more likely cause was **leptospirosis**, a bacterial disease carried by black rats and mice. These rodents escaped from European fishing ships that had worked the North Atlantic coast long before colonization and made their homes in native settlements, contaminating water and food supplies.

Patuxet, where the Pilgrims built their settlement, was one of the villages decimated, which left much of southeastern Massachusetts empty of Native Americans. Because the Wampanoag avoided contact with their enemy—the neighboring Narragansett—the disease was not transmitted to the latter. In a much stronger position, the Narragansett posed an ever-present threat to the weakened Wampanoag Nation.

English and Wampanoag delegations discussed terms of a peace treaty in Plymouth Colony. Those present included Massasoit, leader of the Wampanoag, and Governor John Carver.

agreements with the English. Having access to English goods, particularly weapons, would strengthen his hand.

Massasoit, Peacemaker with an Agenda

The Wampanoag delegation that met with the Pilgrims for the first time in 1621 included Massasoit, who was the sachem of the Wampanoag confederacy, and two interpreters: Samoset, sachem of the Abenaki, and Tisquantum (Squanto), a member of the Patuxet tribe (and a captive whom Massasoit mistrusted). Facing them were Governor John Carver, Edward Winslow, and other prominent colonists. Winslow left this account of Massasoit:

> "In his person he is a very lusty man, in his best years, an able body, grave of countenance, and spare of speech. In his attire little or nothing differing from

the rest of his followers, only in a great chain of white bone beads about his neck, and at it behind his neck hangs a little bag of tobacco, which he drank and gave us to drink; his face was painted with a sad red like murry, and oiled both head and face, that he looked greasily. All his followers likewise, were in their faces, in part or in whole painted, some black, some red, some yellow, and some white, some with crosses, and other antic works; some had skins on them, and some naked, all strong, tall, all men of appearance — [he] had in his bosom hanging in a string, a great long knife; he marveled much at our trumpet, and some of his men would sound it as well as they could."

Wampanoag leader Massasoit was a striking figure who maintained good relations with the colonists.

THE COUNTRYSIDE IN COLONIAL AMERICA

After a ceremonial exchange of greetings and gifts, the leaders negotiated a peace treaty that enabled the sides to coexist without any major conflicts for half a century. Among the terms was the assurance of mutual support in the event of enemy attack.

King Philip's War

Massasoit's alliance with the English helped his people in the short run. But it hurt his relations with tribes who opposed the presence of foreigners. Over the following decades, as the number of colonial towns and villages grew, the indigenous people saw more and more of their land falling into foreign hands. The loss of ancestral land and the threat this posed to their way of life was an inevitable source of conflict.

Massasoit lived into his eighties and died around 1661. For a short time, Wamsutta, his eldest son, replaced him as the Great Sachem. In 1662, his brother, Metacom, became the new sachem. By this time, relations between Native Americans and settlers had seriously eroded. In 1675, the execution of three Wampanoag men by Plymouth colonists outraged young Wampanoag warriors. They struck back at poorly defended settlements. Their victories inspired other groups with their own grievances to join the rebellion, which spread throughout New England.

In response, colonial leaders enlisted the support of Native allies such as the Pequot, Mohegan, and Mohawk. Their fighting skills helped the colonists prevail. King Philip's War, as the colonists called it, ended in the summer of 1676 with the defeat of the resistance and the death of Metacom in battle.

CHAPTER FIVE

Home and Hearth

Pilgrims raced to build shelter against the bitter
Massachusetts winter.

"To greater families we allotted larger plots, to every person half
a pole in breadth, and three in length, and so lots were cast where
every man should lie, which was done, and staked out. We thought
this proportion was large enough at the first for houses and gardens,
to impale them round, considering the weakness of our people,
many of them growing ill with cold, for our former discoveries in
frost and storms, and the wading at Cape Cod had brought much
weakness amongst us, which increased so every day more and more,
and after was the cause of many of their deaths."
—From Mourt's Relation: *A Journal of the Pilgrims at Plymouth*,
entry December 28, 1620

What must it have been like for the first settlers when they
reached North America? No matter what time of year they
arrived, they would have had to battle nature. While Native
Americans would have found comfort and warmth inside
snug houses, the settlers had no such shelters awaiting them.

FINDING SHELTER

One of the first tasks for colonial newcomers was to either find or build
their own shelter. In some instances, the fastest and most expedient course of
action was to dig a cave in a riverbank or hill. This is what some families and
individuals did in places such as Massachusetts, New York, and Pennsylvania,
at least until they had time to build proper houses. While their surroundings
might have contained ample amounts of raw building materials such as wood
and stone, there were no sawmills to transform these materials into useable
commodities. A carefully dug hole in the earth, with a roof made of tree
branches covered with bark or sod, would serve well enough.

Some settlers, upon discovering Native American villages, built their own versions of traditional Native homes. Eventually, colonists throughout British America picked up their broad axes and went to work building log houses. The first step was to find a suitable location and then begin the arduous task of felling trees to make room for a house. Using whatever woodworking tools they brought with them, the colonists cut and shaped enough logs to make the walls and roof.

Once the basic structure was in place, they would need to fill any cracks between the logs with wooden wedges or clay. One settler who failed to seal the cracks in his log house received an unexpected visitor during the night. The visitor was a curious wolf that had shoved his nose through an opening and scratched the sleeping man's head with his teeth.

These early houses were often built on land shared with Native Americans. To protect themselves, colonists enclosed their homes in a sturdy fence built

The Dutch built a protective stockade around their settlement on the island of Manhattan; this site became Wall Street.

from tall, upright timbers fitted side by side. The result was a kind of fort, or **garrison**, which provided shelter in the event of attack.

SEEING IN THE DARK

During colonial times, once the sun went down, the only source of light was a fire. There were no light bulbs and no wall switches that instantly lit up a darkened room. Even starting a fire in the fireplace could be a challenge, since the first practical matches weren't invented until the early 1800s in England. Called *congreves*, they were strips of wood or cardboard coated with sulfur and tipped with a mixture of flammable chemicals.

To ignite a pile of kindling, settlers struck a bit of steel with a piece of flint to produce a spark. The tinder caught the spark, which the appointed fire-starter blew into a flame. It might take several attempts, but eventually the tinder would catch, and the addition of dry wood would yield a cozy fire.

The materials needed to start a fire in this manner were kept in a container called a tinderbox. If the fire went out during the night, someone in the family could carry a shovel or pan to the nearest neighbor's house and borrow enough hot coals to restart the fire.

The fireplace served as a stove for Colonial woman.

For additional light, families relied on candles. Candle making was usually done in the fall when families were preparing for the cold and darkness of winter. To make candles, rows of wicks suspended from rods were repeatedly dipped in kettles of boiling water and melted **tallow**—the fat from parts of certain farm animals. (Tallow could also be made from plants such as bayberry.) Wicks were made from **flax** fibers, twisted cotton, or the downy tufts found in milkweed pods.

Early settlers observed Native Americans burning pitch pine to illuminate their dwellings. Pitch pine trees are also known as candlewood. Referring to pitch pine knots, the Reverend Francis Higginson of Salem, Massachusetts, wrote in 1633 that "They are such candles as the Indians commonly use, having no other, and they are nothing else but the wood of the pine tree, cloven in two little slices, something thin, which are so full of the moysture of turpentine and pitch that they burne as cleere as a torch."

The pitch, or resin, was a kind of tar, which could be used to make turpentine, a valuable product. Once settlers realized the value of pitch pine resin, it became one of colonial America's most important trade items.

With the development of the whaling industry in the eighteenth century, a new kind of fuel was available to colonial homes—the head oil from sperm whales. It was used to make **spermaceti** wax. Candles made from this wax burned slowly and were several times brighter than candles made from tallow.

KITCHEN COMFORT

Even today, the family kitchen tends to be the room where people enjoy gathering, not only to eat but also to socialize. The same was true in the colonial era. In those days, kitchens had large fireplaces for cooking. These fireplaces were also used for heat, since there was no central heating from gas, oil, or electricity. In some rural homes, the fireplace was so enormous that a cook could roast an entire ox over the flames.

Logs for burning had to be dragged inside on a sled or with the aid of horses because of their size and weight. Over time, however, people built smaller fireplaces—mostly because of a shortage of trees as forests were cleared for settlements.

Turnspit dogs kept meat rotating in front of colonial fireplaces.

TURNSPIT DOGS

Imagine running on a wheel for hours at a time so your family could have their cut of meat evenly roasted over an open fire. Performing this task was the job of a special breed of English canines called Turnspit Dogs. At one time, these animals could be found in many colonial and European homes. They were trained to keep a **treadmill** turning by running inside it. The motion of the treadmill turned the spit, or rod, which rotated meat over the fire in a kitchen hearth. The little dog running so fervently inside the wheel had to endure heat and smoke from the fire without stopping to rest. Many died from sheer exhaustion. Fortunately, modern technology long ago eliminated the need for Turnspit Dogs, and the breed has since become extinct.

The typically large fireplace in a colonial farmhouse provided a convenient place for children to sit and read or gaze up through the chimney to a night sky filled with stars. Winter nights, especially in New England and the middle colonies, were sometimes so cold that water left out in unheated bedrooms

Ben Franklin, annoying his family around the fireplace as a boy, invented what we now call the Franklin stove (below). It burned coal and wood.

froze overnight. Even sap forced out of burning logs would freeze if the temperature sufficiently dropped. The sixth president of the United States, John Adams (1735–1826), so dreaded New England winters he wished he could be a dormouse that slept comfortably from fall to spring.

BEATING THE COLD

German immigrants living in Pennsylvania were among the first colonists to use stoves for heating. The design and convenience of these stoves inspired Benjamin Franklin (1706–1790). An inventor and one of the Founding Fathers of this country, Franklin came up with his own version of German stoves. His "New Pennsylvania Fireplace" burned both wood and coal. Dutch and German settlers in the middle colonies generally fared better during the winter, thanks to their use of stoves for heating and featherbeds for sleeping.

Climbing into a cold bed on a winter night was hardly a pleasant experience, so colonists used bed warmers. These were covered copper or brass pans filled with hot coals and connected to a long wooden handle. By sweeping the pan under the covers, a person could instantly warm the sheets before getting in.

Brick Ovens for Baking

For baking, colonial house-wives used brick ovens built into the side of the fireplace chimney. Once a wood fire had heated the oven, the coals and ashes were removed, and the cook slipped a freshly made pie, pot of beans, or loaf of bread into the warm oven. Bread dough was baked in a pan, or sometimes placed on an

The oven peel was a valuable tool in the baking of bread.

arrangement of oak leaves the cook's children had gathered during the autumn. To set the food into the deep-set oven to cook, a long-handled shovel was used, similar to those used by pizza makers, called a peel, or slice. The oven peel was thought to bring good luck, and was often given as a wedding gift to a bride.

Food, Drink, and Table Manners

In many colonial homes, children ate their meals separately from their parents and other adult relatives, and were expected to remain silent during mealtimes. Even when parents allowed their children to join them at the table, they were expected to seat themselves only after the blessing had been made and only with their parents' permission. Tables were usually wooden planks about 3 feet (1 m) wide resting on supports at either end. They might also be made from the chests or packing boxes colonists brought from England.

For seating, people sat on backless benches and ate from **trenchers**—square pieces of wood with a bowl-shaped center for the food. Usually, two people shared one trencher instead of eating from individual plates. Sometimes, in place of trenchers, people ate from bowl-shaped holes carved into the table every 18 inches (46 centimeters) or so. When the meal was over, the table was cleaned so it would be ready for the next meal.

During the seventeenth century, forks were rare. The most commonly used eating utensils were knives and spoons. Many meals consisted of stews and soups made from vegetables and meat. For that reason, spoons were a practical necessity. Because people often handled their food while they ate, they needed lots of napkins to keep their hands clean. As for drinking, it was common for settlers in the countryside to drink from the same vessel. (The discovery that germs could spread infectious diseases wasn't made until the nineteenth century.) Pitchers, cups, and other vessels were made from a variety of materials including wood, leather, animal horns, gourds, and even coconuts. Glass was generally costly or unavailable.

The centerpiece of the typical family table was the salt dispenser, called a salt cellar. Children were usually seated "below the salt," while guests and other important people sat "above the salt," close to the host and hostess. The most popular beverages were cider, rum, tea, coffee, and beer or ale. Colonists tended to avoid drinking ordinary water since in European cities much of the water was polluted and when consumed, caused people to become seriously ill. They feared that in America the water would be just as unhealthy. In the seventeenth century, alcohol was considered much safer. Men, women, children, and even babies drank beer, wine, and ale.

In colonial America, fish and wildlife were plentiful and provided colonists with a ready source of food. Over the years, each region developed its own

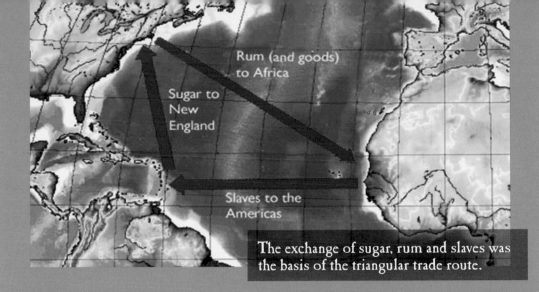

Rum (and goods) to Africa

Sugar to New England

Slaves to the Americas

The exchange of sugar, rum and slaves was the basis of the triangular trade route.

RUM AND NEW ENGLAND'S SLAVE TRADE

Rum is an alcoholic beverage made from fermented sugarcane juice or molasses, a by-product of the **fermentation** process. The popularity of this drink fueled a booming industry in British America beginning in the 1700s. New England, especially the colonies of Massachusetts and Rhode Island, were the heart of this industry. The production process involved a triangular trading system: Ships leaving New England ports laden with barrels of rum sailed to West Africa, where the rum and other goods were traded for African slaves. The slaves were taken to Caribbean islands to work on sugarcane plantations producing sugar and molasses, which were then exported to New England distilleries for making rum.

cuisine based on climate, geography, and local plants and animals. Methods of selecting and preparing foods owed much to British traditions, since the majority of colonists came from the British Isles, which included England, Scotland, Wales, and Ireland. In the New World, colonists could choose from a variety of vegetables such as pumpkins, squash, potatoes, peas, and beans. Once they began harvesting apples, they could make cider, which served as an alternative to alcoholic beverages.

Instead of using maple sugar or honey, a family could purchase loaf sugar to sweeten their food. These loaves weighed up to 10 pounds (4.5 kilograms) and were wrapped in decorative, purple-tinted paper. Colonial housewives wishing to color their homespun wool could use the color in this paper as a dye.

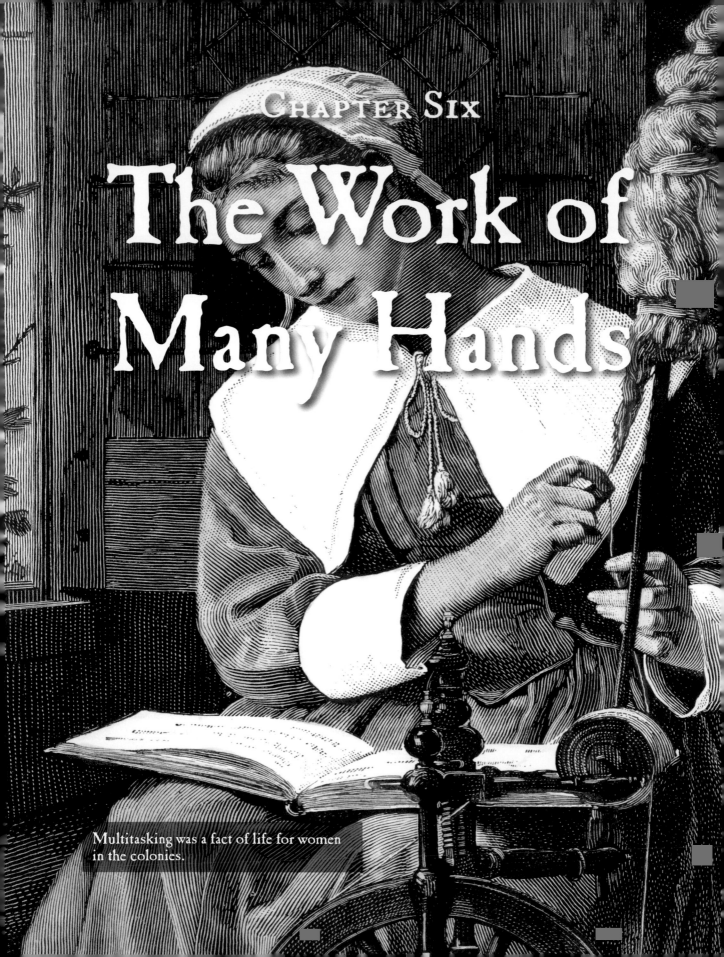

CHAPTER SIX

The Work of Many Hands

Multitasking was a fact of life for women in the colonies.

"Fix'd gown for Prude,—Mend Mother's Riding-hood,—Spun
short thread,—Fix'd two gowns for Welsh's girls,—Carded
tow,—Spun linen,—Worked on Cheese-basket,—Hatchel'd flax
with Hannah, we did 51 lbs. apiece,—Pleated and ironed,—Read
a Sermon of Doddridge's,—Spooled a piece,—Milked the
cows,—Spun linen, did 50 knots,—Made a Broom of Guinea
wheat straw,—Spun thread to whiten,—Set a Red dye,—Had two
Scholars from Mrs. Taylor's,—I carded two pounds of whole wool
and felt Nationly,—Spun harness twine,—Scoured the pewter."
—from the diary of Abigail Foote,
a young girl living in Colchester, Connecticut (1775)

As if Abigail Foote didn't already have more than enough to do, she also handled the washing and cooking, knitted socks and mittens for her family, weeded the garden, and helped her mother make candles and soap during certain times of the year. Abigail's life was typical of the way many women lived in colonial America. Life was hard, and every member of the family had to lend a hand to make sure the work was done.

Most colonists were farmers, and maintaining a farm in the different regions of the colonies required a great deal of backbreaking labor. Families tended to be large—more children meant more hands for all the jobs that needed doing. As in Native American villages, gender influenced the sort of work family members did. In general, men and boys were responsible for clearing the land, putting up fences, building stone walls and livestock pens, cutting firewood, and other types of heavy labor. They might also hunt and fish in addition to growing food for their families.

TYPES OF WORK IN COLONIAL TOWNS

Men who lived in towns or cities usually worked in one of the many crafts and trades. In those days, everything had to be made by hand, since the factory system and mass production were far in the future. Boys could undertake an **apprenticeship** with a master tradesman and acquire on-the-job training for a period of four to seven years or longer. Instead of wages, the apprentice would receive lodging, meals, and clothing from this master. At the end of his training, a young man was qualified to begin his own business. In colonial cities, there was always a demand for blacksmiths, shoemakers, tailors, weavers, and other skilled workers.

WOMEN'S WORK

In the countryside, it must have seemed that a woman's work was never done. Besides tending the fire and preparing meals, a woman might have to work in the fields along with the men, take care of the children, tend the family garden, clean the house, make soap and candles, and administer remedies for common ailments. On top of these tasks, women were also responsible for teaching their daughters the skills they would need once they married and had children of their own. Following in their mothers' footsteps, girls learned to cook, milk the cows, operate a butter churn, make cheese, preserve food, spin, knit, sew, and weave.

Women required many skills to care for their families.

But not all women devoted their days to housework and childcare. Recent research has shown that in colonial times, women worked in most of the same trades as men. For instance, there were women shoemakers, weavers, spinners, seamstresses, and wig makers. They also managed the farm whenever their husbands were absent for any length of time.

Conditions required that females do tasks that fell outside of what was considered women's work.

Some women worked in what were considered strictly male occupations such as blacksmithing or running a tavern or inn. In the eighteenth century, Christina Campbell operated a tavern in Williamsburg, Virginia. She was such an accomplished proprietor that her establishment was George Washington's favorite place to dine in Williamsburg.

THE STORY OF MARY JEMISON

The unending hardship of rural life in British America prompted some settlers to view the Native American way of life as much more agreeable. The historical record contains reports of colonial women who became part of native communities and had little desire to return to their former way of life.

The story of Mary Jemison is an example of this migration from one world to another. Mary was born in 1743 to Scots-Irish immigrants. Her family settled in

THE STATUS OF COLONIAL WOMEN

Colonial society was **patriarchal**. Married women had few rights. Only men could vote, own land, and serve in the church as a minister or other member of the clergy. By tradition, fathers had the final word when it came to making decisions for the family. The reality was probably more complex. More likely than not, some wives shared authority with their spouses. Widows, on the other hand, enjoyed certain rights not available to married women. They were entitled to own a share of their late husband's property and, in some colonies, they could vote.

the frontier land of what was then western Pennsylvania, not far from Gettysburg. When Mary was a teenager, the French and Indian War was underway. The war was actually between France and England over possession of North American territory. Both sides enlisted Native American allies to help them.

In 1758, French soldiers and Shawnee warriors came upon the Jemisons' cabin. Mary's two oldest brothers escaped, but she, her parents, and her other siblings were taken captive. Their captors decided to keep just Mary and her neighbor's son. Separated from her family, she was turned over to members of the Seneca tribe. That tribe adopted her and gave her a new name—"Dehgewanus," translated as "Two Falling Voices." Later, she married a Seneca man with whom she had a child. For the rest of her life, Dehgewanus remained by choice with the Seneca people. She died in 1833 while living on the Buffalo Creek Indian Reservation in New York.

Communities came together so people didn't have to always work alone.

BUILDING A COMMUNITY IN THE COUNTRYSIDE

To lighten the load of constant work in the colonial countryside, settlers pooled resources and cooperated with each other. Besides making the work easier, cooperation strengthened the sense of community and provided opportunities for socializing and entertainment. In order to survive in rural areas, settlers had to depend not only on themselves and their families but also on their neighbors. For instance, when a new family moved into a settlement, folks got together to help clear the ground for the family's home and farm. A term for this cooperative enterprise was "log rolling." People also helped each other "raise" a house, barn, church, or schoolhouse. Young and old, men and women—all were invited to lend a hand to get the job done.

"Breaking out" was another way in which neighbors worked together to accomplish what one person alone would have a hard time doing. During the winter, when deep snowfalls made roads impassable, neighbors gathered with teams of oxen. Pulling heavy plows, the oxen cleared the snow. The poet John Greenleaf Whittier, in a part of his poem "Snow-Bound," describes a typical "breaking out":

> Next morn we wakened with the shout
> Of merry voices high and clear;
> And saw the teamsters drawing near
> To break the drifted highways out.
> Down the long hillside treading slow
> We saw the half-buried oxen go,
> Shaking the snow from heads uptost,
> Their straining nostrils white with frost.
> Before our door the straggling train
> Drew up, an added team to gain.
> The elders threshed their hands a-cold,
> Passed, with the cider mug, their jokes
> From lip to lip.

In settlements with common lands on which farmers grazed livestock, men often looked after each other's animals, taking them to and from the pasture. In New England, where the soil was rocky, people would work together to remove the rocks and use them to build stone walls.

"Change work" was a more modest form of cooperation. A few women friends getting together to make soap, for example, was considered "change work." Women also met to sew **quilts** in quilting bees, which are still cooperative activities in some communities today.

In the Pennsylvania countryside, German immigrants continued the old world custom of slaughtering cattle in the fall and making sausages from the meat. (Sausage soup in German is *metzelsuppe*.) Part of the custom was to send bowls of sausage soup to close friends and neighbors with the expectation that they would do the same in return. But if someone failed to send back a bowl of soup, tempers sometimes flared, feelings were hurt, and the local minister would occasionally have to step in to make peace between offended neighbors.

CHAPTER SEVEN

Childhood in the Countryside

Childhood was a precarious time in the colonies, which experienced high mortality rates among the young.

"We have our children taken from us, the Desire of our Eyes taken away with a stroke."
—Minister Cotton Mather, who lost eight children before they reached the age of two

In 1630, ten years after the Pilgrims landed on the shores of Massachusetts, a larger group of British immigrants made the same voyage. Their new colony was Massachusetts Bay, which was located about 40 miles (64 km) north of the Plymouth Colony, founded by the Pilgrims. This second group of settlers reached Massachusetts in June. After two months at sea, the passengers enjoyed "a smell on the shore like the smell of a garden," according to John Winthrop (1588–1649), the first governor of Massachusetts Bay Colony.

THREATS TO SURVIVAL

Some of the women and children gathered wild roses and fresh strawberries as they explored their new home. The children must have been especially happy to be on dry land instead of inside a cramped, cold ship. But the days that followed would prove even more challenging than their time at sea. Life in the colonies was anything but a "bed of roses." Many children didn't survive; they died while still young from disease or malnutrition. Missing the benefits of modern medical science, parents relied on folk remedies and a dose of superstition to keep their kids healthy.

Mortality was very high. The average marriage lasted only twelve years, and one third to one half of all children lost a parent before the age of twenty-one. This problem was worse in the South, where more than half of all children under the age of fourteen lost at least one parent.

One of the main causes was difficulty with childbirth. There were no hospitals, so most children were born at home. If a woman was lucky, she would have the assistance of a **midwife**. In the South, the majority of midwives were African American slaves serving on plantations. In the North, access to a midwife was found mostly in the cities. The first paid midwife was employed in 1660 by New Amsterdam to treat the poor. In the seventeenth and eighteenth centuries in colonial America, between one and one and a half percent of all births ended with the mother dying. The causes were exhaustion, dehydration, infection, hemorrhage, or convulsions.

Fathers often served as pharmacists for their families.

Because a mother typically had five to eight children, her chances of dying in childbirth could be as high as one in eight. This high death rate meant that people frequently got remarried. In Plymouth, the first marriage of record was between a man who had been widowed just seven weeks and a woman whose husband had died just twelve weeks earlier.

An adult could expect not only to lose a spouse during his or her lifetime, but also one or more children. In a diary kept by Samuel Sewall from 1673 to 1729, it was recorded that seven of his fourteen children died before the age of two. The famous preacher, Cotton Mather, lost eight of his fifteen children before they reached the age of two.

In the seventeenth century, medical science was still influenced by a widespread belief in **astrology** and other pre-Christian practices. The month in which a child was born, the phase of the moon, the alignment of the planets—these were considered factors that could affect a child's health and the path he would follow in life.

Knowing the astrological conditions under which a child was born might also determine which medicines were used to treat a particular kind of sickness.

These medicines, for the most part, were concoctions of natural ingredients that may or may not have been beneficial. Some of them probably did more harm than good.

A popular household remedy was Snail Water, used mostly by those unable to afford more expensive treatments. In the early 1700s, a London doctor came up with a recipe for Snail Water that included ordinary garden snails, earthworms, various herbs and spices, and seeds and berries. Modern **herbalists** who have tested this mixture report that some of the ingredients actually do have medicinal properties.

Venice Treacle was another cure-all used by colonists for children as well as adults. The origin of this compound goes as far back as the ancient Greeks. It remained in use until the middle of the eighteenth century, though the recipe has varied through the centuries. In colonial times, Venice Treacle was made from **opium**, licorice, red roses, an assortment of herbs and spices, some honey, and several venomous snakes soaked in wine.

Popular in England and the United States, Daffy's Elixir was a patent medicine invented in the mid-1600s by Thomas Daffy, a British clergyman. It was advertised as a cure for all sorts of ailments, including stomach disorders in children.

COLD FEET, WARM BEER, AND CANDY

The seventeenth-century British philosopher and physician John Locke published a book about raising children, titled *Thought on Education*, in 1690. His advice greatly influenced—rightly or wrongly—generations of parents in colonial America. Locke believed that parents should wash their children's feet in cold water at least once a day. He also advised that their shoes should be so thin that water could easily soak through. Josiah Quincy, a New England colonist, recalled that from the time he was three years old, his parents dutifully followed Locke's instructions. Every morning, they plunged his feet in a tub of cold water even during the coldest months of the year. Oddly enough, Quincy never got sick from having cold, wet feet while growing up.

Locke had some tips about what foods growing children should and should not eat. He ruled out certain fruits such as melons, peaches, plums, and grapes but thought apples, pears, and berries were good. For breakfast and supper, Locke wrote, children would be well-advised to eat brown bread with cheese or milk served with gruel, a watery porridge. Warm beer, he wrote, should also be part of a child's diet. However, in colonial America, children tended to drink more milk than beer. They also ate cereal dishes their mothers learned to make from Native American women, who used corn in much of their cooking.

Candies such as sugar crystals made from sugarcane were available to colonial children.

Sweets were readily available in the colonies, thanks to the overseas trade. Ships sailing into seaport harbors carried cargoes of sugar, molasses, ginger, chocolate, and dried fruits such as raisins. Strings of clear rock candy from China were as eagerly consumed as maple sugar treats made in the colonies. All in all, there was no shortage of candies for colonial kids, especially those who lived in or near seaport towns like Boston, Salem, and New York. Native American adults and children processed the sap from maple trees to make maple sugar, which Eastern Woodland Native Americans traded with the settlers.

Infants, Toddlers, and Beyond

The first colonists in America often gave names to their newborns that were found in the Bible, inspired by the circumstances of the parents' lives at the time of birth, or based on the hopes they had for the children. In one family, the father was a doctor who perished in a snowstorm while attempting to visit a sick neighbor. The doctor's wife named their newborn daughter Fathergone in remembrance of his untimely death. New England Puritans often chose names that expressed virtues or character traits they greatly valued, such as Patience, Charity, Faith, Love, Endurance, and Silence.

In industrial regions of the world today, childhood is a time of discovery free from the responsibilities of adulthood. Young people spend most of their days in school preparing for later life. In this country, child labor laws require a person to be fourteen before he or she can legally work. These laws also spell out the conditions under which minors sixteen and younger may hold a job.

Even young children had to help with household chores.

During colonial times, however, childhood was short-lived. From a young age, boys and girls were expected to behave like adults and to contribute their share of labor for the good of the family.

Most white children were educated at home by their parents; little to no schooling was provided for the Native Americans or for the slaves. Boys were taught a range of subjects, with those of the wealthier classes learning classic texts, languages such as Latin and Greek, higher math, and sciences to prepare them for the top

Fathers were often the first teachers for their children.

schools in England. Girls were taught subjects such as reading and arithmetic—things they needed to run a household.

In the South, on tobacco plantations, children picked leaf-eating caterpillars off the tobacco leaves. After they were picked, children crushed them between their fingers to make sure the tiny insects didn't continue munching on the plants.

During the spring, throughout the colonies, small children helped out by sowing seeds. Little girls did much of the spinning, even when they were so small they had to stand on a stool to reach the spinning wheel. Most farms had fields of flax, a plant whose fibers can be spun into thread or yarn. While fathers and sons cultivated the fields and gathered the fibers, mothers and daughters did the spinning. Everyone then pitched in to weave the yarn into cloth, which was then used to make clothing for the entire family.

Rural families also had their own flocks of sheep. After the sheep were sheared in the spring, the wool could be woven on a wool wheel. Many families kept both a wool wheel and a flax wheel in their kitchen.

In some colonies, children tending sheep were required by law to busy themselves in some additional occupation while watching over the flock. Children learned from an early age that keeping busy and staying useful were the hallmarks of responsible adults. While in school, they were to concentrate on their studies; after school, there were chores to do till the sun went down. Watering the horses, feeding the livestock, chopping firewood, carrying in vegetables from the garden—these were some of the tasks children were expected to perform at home.

Bowling was among the games brought from Europe to North America.

Fun and Games

You might very well conclude that colonial children were overworked and "underplayed." But even with all the chores they had to do, they still found time to enjoy themselves. Some of their favorite activities have survived into the present—games such as tag, hide-and-seek, hopscotch, kite flying, leapfrog, marbles, blind man's bluff, and jumping rope.

In the winter, kids went sledding and skating. They also played cat's cradle with yarn or thread, still a popular pastime for pairs of children.

Like children around the world, children in colonial America recited rhymes and sang songs while playing. Many of their songs have been passed down by word-of-mouth from one generation of children to the next. Songs such as "Ring Around the Rosie," "London Bridge Is Falling Down," and "Here We Go Round the Mulberry Bush" have a long history that link the present with the past—making colonial America seem not so distant after all.

Glossary

apprenticeship

On-the-job training during which a young person works under a master tradesman or craftsman. In colonial times, an apprentice would live with the master's family and receive food, lodging, and clothing in place of wages.

aristocracy

People who belong to the highest social class and enjoy considerable wealth and privilege.

astrology

The study of the planets and other heavenly bodies in the belief that their positions and aspects influence human lives.

blockhouse

A fortified building with portholes through which soldiers could shoot muskets; otherwise known as a fort or garrison.

clan

A group of people from common descent; family.

cuisine

The types of food and ways of preparing them that are characteristic of a region or country.

epidemic

An outbreak of contagious disease that infects a great many people living in the same general area.

fermentation

The process by which certain microscopic organisms break down carbohydrates into simpler substances. What is produced through fermentation depends on the type of microorganism carrying on the process and the medium that is used. For instance, when yeast ferments in grain, the end result is the alcohol and carbonation in beer.

flax

A plant highly valued for its seeds and the fibers contained in its stems. The fiber of the flax plant can be used to make linen cloth.

garrison

A military fort in which soldiers are stationed. In the colonial era, garrisons provided a refuge for civilians under attack by hostile Native Americans.

herbalist

Someone who knows a great deal about herbs, especially their medicinal benefits.

immigrants

A person who moves to another country, usually for permanent residence.

indentured servant

During colonial times, an indentured servant was someone who agreed to work without pay for a certain period of time in exchange for free passage to America. In some cases, indentured servitude was a form of bondage that left the person with few rights.

leptospirosis

A severe infection caused by exposure to a certain strain of bacteria in the urine of infected animals.

longhouse

The traditional shelter of Eastern Woodland Native Americans.

matriarchal

In a culture, society, or tribe that is matriarchal, women are the dominant authority.

midwife

A person trained to assist a woman during childbirth.

mock

Pretend. Not real or authentic.

opium

An addictive drug once used as a painkiller.

patriarchal

A patriarchal culture, society, or tribe is one in which men are the dominant authority.

plantation

Early in the colonial period, the word "plantation" meant "colony." Later, it came to mean a large estate or farm on which crops are grown for export.

Puritans

Members of the Protestant Church of England who believed the Church had not gone far enough in removing the influence of Roman Catholic rituals and doctrines. Puritans who wanted to leave the Church and set up their own independent congregations were known as "Separatists." One group of Separatists left England in 1620 and settled in Massachusetts. We know them today as the Pilgrims.

quilt

A blanket or bedspread with wool or cotton padding between two layers of fabric. The fabric is held in place by a decorative stitching pattern.

sachem

The chief or leader of an Eastern Woodland tribe or alliance of tribes.

Saints

The Protestant Separatists who sailed to New England aboard the *Mayflower* referred to themselves as "Saints," not "Pilgrims."

spermaceti

A fluid found in the head of a sperm whale or bottlenose whale. It was once used to make wax candles and as an ingredient in cosmetics and ointments.

subjugate

To dominate or make someone subservient.

subordinate

To place someone in an inferior or less important position.

tallow

The fat obtained from certain plants or the bodies of animals like sheep, horses, or cattle. Colonial women used tallow to make candles.

treadmill

A device upon which a person or animal walks or runs in place.

trencher

A square block of wood with a bowl-shaped center for holding food.

wetu/wetuash

The singular and plural forms of the Wampanoag word for "house." Wampanoag houses were round and made from cattail mats or sheets of bark arranged over a wooden frame.

Further Reading

Nonfiction

Gray, Edward C. *Colonial America: A History in Documents*. Pages from History. New York, NY: Oxford University Press, 2011.

Lassieur, Allison. *Colonial America: An Interactive History Adventure*. You Choose: Historical Eras. Mankato, MN: You Choose Books, 2011.

Lombard, Anne, and Middleton, Richard. *Colonial America, A History to 1763*. Malden, MA: Wiley-Blackwell, 2011.

Fiction

Kudlinski, Katherine V. *My Lady Pocahontas*. Amazon Children's Publishing, Skyscape, 2013.

Lenski, Lois. *Indian Captive: The Story of Mary Jemison*. New York, NY: HarperCollins Publishers, 1995.

Sedgwick, Maria Catherine. *Hope Leslie: or Early Times in Massachusetts*. Mineola, NY: Dover Publications, Inc., 2011.

Websites

Colonial America (1492–1763)

The Library of Congress

www.americaslibrary.gov/jb/colonial/jb_colonial_subj.html

From the Library of Congress in Washington, D.C., this kid-friendly website offers young readers an engaging look at America's past, including true stories about the country's colonial era from 1492 to 1763.

Colonial Life in Early America

Kid Info

www.kidinfo.com/american_history/colonization_colonial_life.html
This site is packed with fascinating information about colonial clothing, foods, medicine, and music, as well as religion, education, and African American life in the colonial era.

Colonial Settlement (1492–1763)

The Library of Congress

www.loc.gov/teachers/additionalresources/relatedresources/ushist/chrono/colonial.html
Teachers as well as students will discover links to websites covering many aspects of colonial times. Interactive elements, primary sources, and videos are among the many resources available through this digital portal to the past.

SELECTED BIBLIOGRAPHY

Boyer, Paul S., ed. *The Oxford Companion to United States History*. New York, NY: Oxford University Press, 2001.

Chapin, Bradly. *Early America*. Englewood, NJ: Jerome S. Ozer Pub, 1984.

Earle, Morse Alice. *Child Life in Colonial Days*. New York, NY: The Macmillan Company, 1915. (Also, a Project Gutenberg eBook released in 2013.)

Earle, Morse Alice. *Home Life in Colonial Days*. Stockbridge, MA: The Berkshire Traveller Press, 1898. (Also, a Project Gutenberg eBook released in 2007.)

Foner, Eric, and Garraty, John A., eds. *The Reader's Companion to American History*. Boston, MA: Houghton Mifflin Company, 1991.

Gray, Edward G. *Colonial America: A History in Documents*. New York, NY: Oxford University Press, Inc., 2003.

Hawke, David Freeman. *Everyday Life in Early America*. New York, NY: Harper & Row, Publishers, 1988.

Miller, John C. *The First Frontier: Life in Colonial America*. Lanham, MD: University Press of America, Inc., 1966.

Smith, Carter, ed. *Daily Life: A Sourcebook on Colonial America*. Brookfield, CT: The Millbrook Press, Inc., 1991.

Snell, Tee Loftin. *The Wild Shores: America's Beginnings*. The National Geographic Society, 1983.

Stile, T. J., ed. *In Their Own Words: The Colonizers*. New York, NY: Penguin Group USA, 1998.

Taylor, Alan. *American Colonies*. New York, NY: Viking Penguin, 2001.

Taylor, Dale. *Writer's Guide to Everyday Life in Colonial America*. Cincinnati, OH: Writer's Digest Books, 1997.

Wallenfeldt, Jeff, ed. *From Columbus To Colonial America: 1492 to 1763*. New York, NY: Britannica Educational Publishing in association with Rosen Educational Services, LLC, 2012.

Quotation Sources

Chapter 1: Struggle for Survival

p. 7, Bradford, William and Edward Winslow, "Mourt's Relation: A Journal of the Pilgrims at Plymouth," retrieved March 14, 2014 from www.histarch.illinois.edu/plymouth/mourt1.html

p. 9, Bradford, William, "Of Plymouth Plantation," retrieved January 10, 2014 from mith.umd.edu//eada/html/display.php?docs=bradford_history.xml

p. 10, Bradford, William and Edward Winslow, "Bradford and Winslow's Journal: An Excursion up Cape Cod," retrieved January 10, 2014 from www.bartleby.com/400/prose/27.html

p. 10, American History from Revolution to Reconstruction and Beyond, "The Colonial Period," retrieved January 9, 2014 from www.let.rug.nl/usa/outlines/history-1954/the-colonial-period.php

p. 10, American History from Revolution to Reconstruction and Beyond, "The Colonial Period."

Chapter 2: People of the Eastern Woodlands

p. 17, de Champlain, Samuel, "'The Iroquois were much astonished that two men should have been killed so quickly': Samuel de Champlain Introduces Firearms to Native Warfare, 1609," retrieved March 14, 2014 from http://historymatters.gmu.edu/d/6594

p. 21, New York State Museum, "Original Descriptions of Iroquois Longhouses by Early European Explorers," retrieved January 15, 2014 from http://www.nysm.nysed.gov/IroquoisVillage/accounts.html

Chapter 3: Jamestown and the Powhatan People

p. 25, Smith, John, "'The Starving Time': John Smith Recounts the Early History of Jamestown, 1609," retrieved March 14, 2014 from historymatters.gmu.edu/d/6593

p. 25, The National Archives, "Source 4: Transcript of extract from a journal of one of the settlers (CO1/1)," retrieved January 17, 2004 from http://www.nationalarchives.gov.uk/documents/education/native-north-americans.pdf

p. 29, Taylor, Alan. *American Colonies*, "Virginia, 1570-1650" (New York: Penguin Books, 2001), p. 131.

p. 31, Taylor, *American Colonies*, pp. 130-131.

p. 31, Taylor, *American Colonies*, p. 131.

p. 32, EyeWitness to History, "Captain Smith is Saved by Pocahontas," retrieved January 29, 2014 from www.eyewitnesstohistory.com/johnsmith.htm

p. 32, EyeWitness to History, "Captain Smith is Saved by Pocahontas."

p. 34, EyeWitness to History, "Captain Smith is Saved by Pocahontas."

Chapter 4: Plymouth Plantation and the Wampanoag

p. 37, Bradford, "Of Plymouth Plantation."

p. 40, Cline, Duane A., "The Wampanoag/Pilgrim Treaty," retrieved January 29, 2014 from www.rootsweb.ancestry.com/~mosmd/peacetreaty.htm

Chapter 5: Home and Hearth

p. 43, Bradford and Winslow, "Mourt's Relation: A Journal of the Pilgrims at Plymouth."

p. 46, Beardsley, John, ed., "A Short and True Description of New England by the Rev. Francis Higginson, 1629," retrieved January 8, 2014 from www.winthropsociety.com/doc_higgin.php

Chapter 6: The Work of Many Hands

p. 53, Crowell, Katherine R., *The Call of the Waters: A Study of the Frontier*, (Google Books) pp. 86-87, retrieved January 30, 2014 from books.google.com/books?id=DqWfjoxxlpoC&pg=PA86&lpg=PA86&dq=Abigail+Foote+diary+excerpts&source=bl&ots=3LToYDQcWX&sig=udpk9oW0atw9VVJV_o9dp3Wi9C4&hl=en&sa=X&ei=DzPwUoyzJfOmsQSswYGwAw&ved=0CE4Q6AEwCQ#v=onepage&q=Abigail%20Foote%20diary%20excerpts&f=false

p. 57, Whittier, John G., "Snow-Bound: A Winter Idyl," retrieved January 30, 2014, www.poetryfoundation.org/poem/174758

Chapter 7: Childhood in the Countryside

p. 59, Earle, Alice Morse, *Child Life in Colonial Days*, (a Gutenberg.org ebook), retrieved March 14, 2014 from www.gutenberg.org/files/43863/43863-h/43863-h.htm

p. 59, Savage, James, ed.,"Shipboard Journal of John Winthrop," retrieved January 13, 2014 from www.winthropsociety.com/journal.php

Index

Page numbers in **boldface** are images.

African Americans, 12–14, 60
apprenticeship, 54
aristocracy, 29
astrology, 61–68

blockhouse, 11

clan, 22
cuisine, 51

diseases
    dysentery, 31
    malaria, 31
    plague, 38
    smallpox, 38
    typhoid fever, 31
    viral hepatitis, 38
    yellow fever, 38
    See also, epidemic; leptospirosis

epidemic, 38

fermentation, 51
flax, 46, 53, 65–66

garrison, 45

herbalist, 62

immigrants, 4–5, 15, 31, 48, 55, 57, 59
indentured servant, 12–14, **13**

leptospirosis, 38
longhouse, **16**, 18–20, **21**, 22–23, 28, **30**, 32

matriarchal, 22
midwife, 60
mock, 34

Native Americans, 10, 12, 14, 28–29, 32–33, 35, 37–38, 41, 43–44, 46, 63
    Eastern Woodland, 15, 17–18, **17**, 27
    schooling, 64
    Six Nations, 18–19, **21**

Author Biography

George Capaccio has been a poet, artist, educator, and writer. A native New Englander, he graduated from the University of Massachusetts with a Bachelor of Arts degree in English literature. Capaccio's books of historical nonfiction include a study of Spanish colonial institutions in North America, ancient trade routes in the Middle East, growing up in the Middle Ages, and the effects of the Black Death on European society. He has also written a middle school test preparation book on U.S. history from the American Revolution to the period of Reconstruction after the Civil War.